Migration

by Robin Nelson

first step nonfiction

Lerner Publications Company · Minneapolis

Many animals move from one home to another.

They move with the **seasons**.

These birds live in one
place for part of the year.

Then they go to live in another place for part of the year.

This **cycle** is called **migration**.

A cycle is a pattern that
happens over and over again.

In the fall, birds migrate
south to warmer places.

In the spring, they migrate
back north.

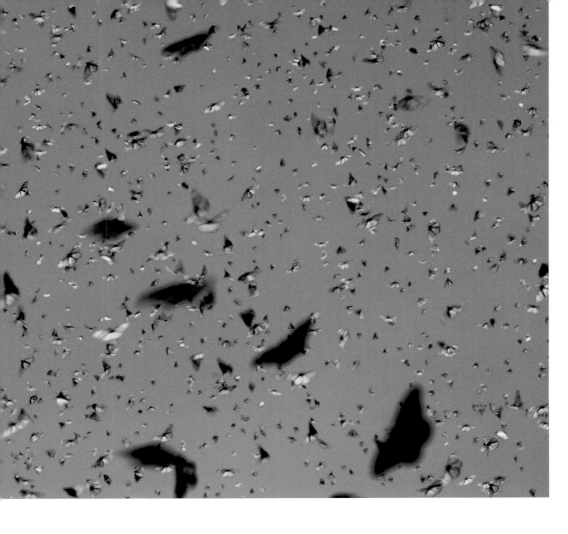

Monarch butterflies also migrate to keep warm.

Some fly from Canada all the way to Mexico.

In the spring, whales migrate
to cold water to eat.

In the fall, they swim to warm water to have families.

Salmon are born in rivers
and migrate to the ocean.

They migrate back to the river to have their young.

Many animals migrate from place to place.

They migrate to find food or to have young.

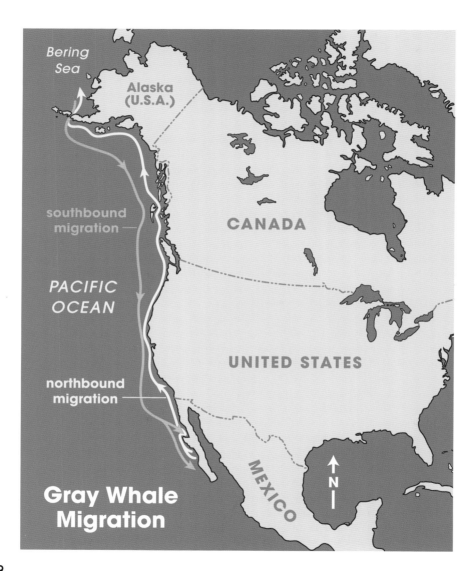

Gray Whale Migration

Learn More about Gray Whale Migration

Every year, gray whales migrate from the ocean near Mexico to the waters off Alaska. They swim about 12,000 miles round-trip! They spend the summer eating in the waters near Alaska. In the winter, they migrate to the ocean near Mexico, where the water is warmer. Gray whale babies are born there.

Migration Facts

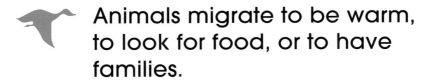

Animals migrate to be warm, to look for food, or to have families.

Most birds migrate in flocks, or groups, of birds.

Caribou, or reindeer, migrate in a group called a herd.

Gray whales migrate the longest distance.

Gray whales migrate in groups called pods.

Every year, monarch butterflies land in the same trees in Mexico.

When monarch butterflies migrate, they fly alone during the day. They rest in groups at night.

Glossary

 cycle – a pattern that happens over and over again

 migration – moving from one place to another to find food or to have young

 salmon – large fish that often have pink or reddish skin

 seasons – the four parts of the year—spring, summer, fall, and winter

Index

The images in this book are used with the permission of: © Flirt/SuperStock, p. 2; © Mark Carwardine/naturepl.com, p. 3; © Gerry Lemmo, pp. 4, 5, 8, 17, 22 (second from top, bottom); © Barry Mansell/SuperStock, pp. 6, 22 (top); © age fotostock/SuperStock, pp. 7, 11, 12, 13, 16; © Karlene Schwartz, p. 9; © Joseph Van Os/The Image Bank/Getty Images, p. 10; © Richard Herrmann/Visuals Unlimited/Getty Images, pp. 14, 22 (second from bottom); © Cusp/SuperStock, p. 15; © Laura Westlund/Independent Picture Service, p. 18.

Front Cover: © iStockphoto.com/Stephen Strathdee.

Lerner Publications Company
A division of Lerner Publishing Group, Inc.
241 First Avenue North
Minneapolis, MN 55401 U.S.A.

Website address: www.lernerbooks.com

Library of Congress Cataloging-in-Publication Data

Nelson, Robin, 1971–
    Migration / by Robin Nelson.
      p. cm. — (First step nonfiction. Discovering nature's cycles)
    Includes index.
    ISBN 978–0–7613–4580–0 (lib. bdg. : alk. paper)
    1. Animal migration—Juvenile literature. I. Title.
QL754.N45 2011
591.56'8—dc22   2009015248

Manufactured in the United States of America
1 – DP – 7/15/10